ROOSTERS

ANN RUFFELL

The Grand Bristleton Easter Egg

illustrated by
Joseph Sharples

HODDER AND STOUGHTON
London Sydney Auckland Toronto

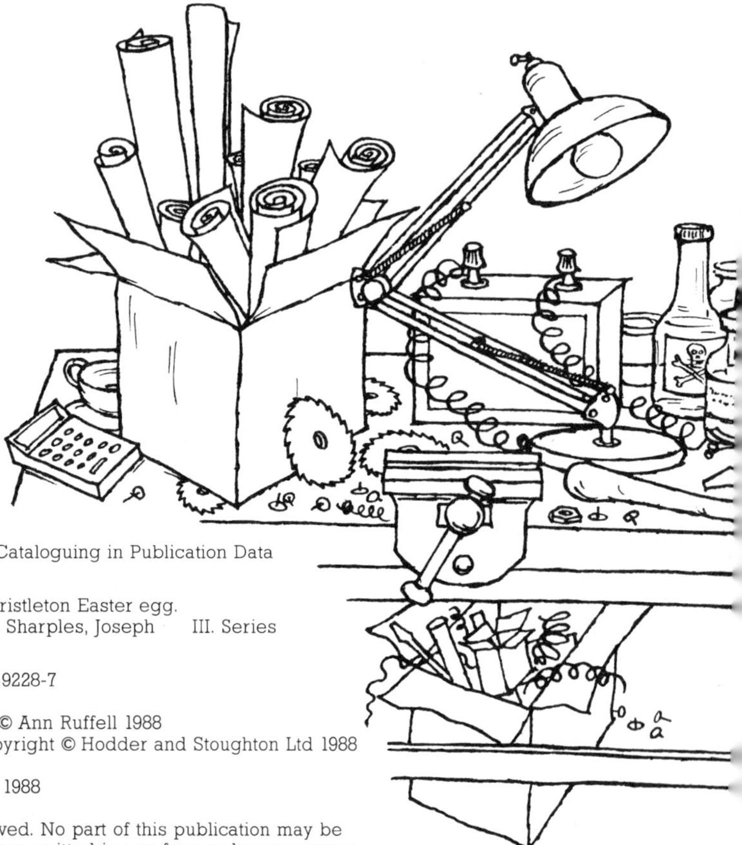

British Library Cataloguing in Publication Data

Ruffell, Ann
The grand Bristleton Easter egg.
I. Title II. Sharples, Joseph III. Series
823'.914[J]

ISBN 0-340-49228-7

First published 1988

Published by Hodder and Stoughton Children's Books,
a division of Hodder and Stoughton Ltd,
Mill Road, Dunton Green, Sevenoaks, Kent TN13 2YJ

Photoset by En to En, Tunbridge Wells, Kent

Printed in Great Britain by T.J. Press (Padstow) Ltd,
Padstow, Cornwall

1 The Easter Egg Surprise

Professor Fred was an inventor.

Her name was not really Fred. It was Felicia Rowanna Euphemia Doreen, but this was too much to shout all at once, so everyone called her Fred for short.

Every year Professor Fred stopped inventing things and made a Grand Easter Egg for all the children of Bristleton instead.

On Easter Sunday the Bristleton children woke up to find chocolate Easter eggs on

their breakfast tables. Then they put on their best clothes and went to church. After lunch they ate their Easter eggs and watched television, just like anyone else.

But Easter Monday was different. On Easter Monday the Bristleton football team played a game of football with their deadly rivals, the Bompton football team. All the people in the town turned out to watch.

The next nice thing on Easter Monday was the Grand Opening of the Grand Easter Egg.

If Bristleton football team had won, it was like an extra prize.

If Bristleton football team had lost, it was something to cheer everyone up.

This year they were playing at home. And this year the Egg was to be bigger and grander than ever before. It was going to fill the Town Hall, right up to the ceiling.

Professor Fred was Little Fred's granny. Little Fred was the only person allowed to see the Egg being made. And only Professor Fred and Little Fred knew what was going to go inside.

It was Easter Sunday. After lunch Little Fred put on his old clothes and went to see his granny, who lived next door.

'Ready, Fred?' said Professor Fred.

'Right ho, Granny,' said Little Fred.

She gave him a bag to carry. Then she lifted another bag and opened the door.

They tiptoed through the town to the Town Hall. Nobody heard them go, because everyone was watching television and eating Easter eggs.

Inside the bags were the things that were going to go inside the Grand Easter Egg. Every year it was something different. This year there were to be thousands of little chocolate elephants, all different flavours. Each one had its owner's name on it, three each. And when the Egg was opened the elephants were going to march out and trumpet the Bristleton Football Club song in four parts.

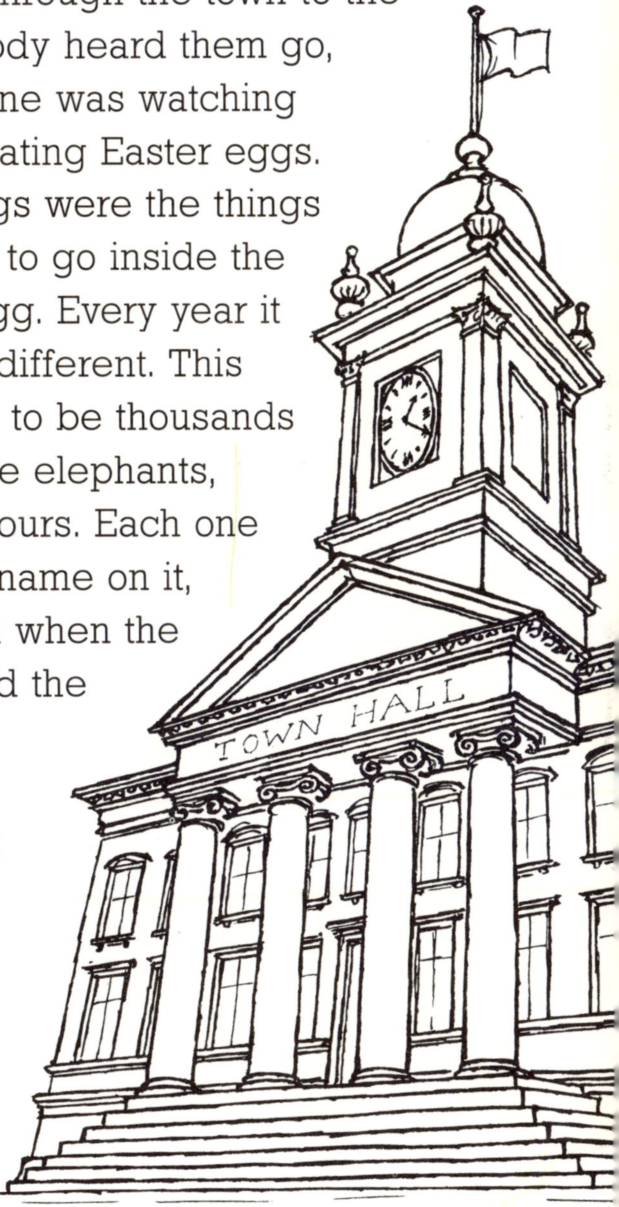

The chocolate eggshells lay like two huge boats on the floor of the Town Hall.

'Are the elephants all wound up?' asked Little Fred.

'Every last one,' said Professor Fred.

Inside each elephant Professor Fred had placed a clockwork engine made of extremely hard sugar, so that when you ate it you didn't get tummy-ache. It had taken her a week to wind them all up.

Little Fred piled thousands of chocolate elephants into his half eggshell, and Professor Fred piled thousands of chocolate elephants into her half. Then they stuck the two halves together and

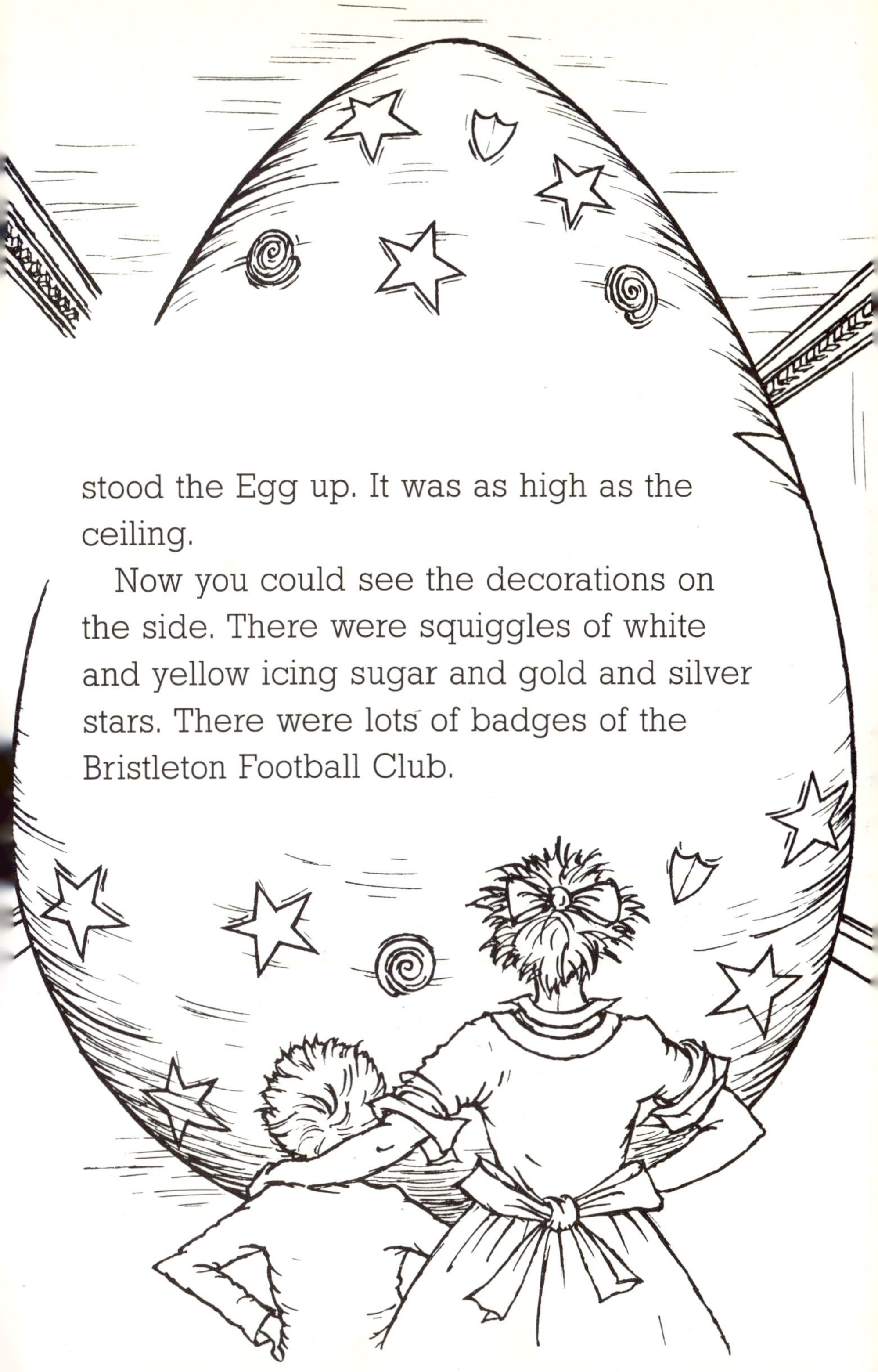

stood the Egg up. It was as high as the ceiling.

Now you could see the decorations on the side. There were squiggles of white and yellow icing sugar and gold and silver stars. There were lots of badges of the Bristleton Football Club.

'Okay, Fred,' said Professor Fred. 'Help me with this ribbon.'

'Right ho, Granny,' said Little Fred, and took his end of the white and yellow

ribbon. These were the Bristleton football team colours.

They tied the ribbon into an enormous bow round the Egg's fat middle.

'That looks pretty good, Fred,' said Professor Fred. 'Roll on tomorrow and opening time.'

'Not half,' said Little Fred.

They shook hands and took a last look. Then they switched off the lights, locked up, and went home to bed.

So they didn't hear the funny noise that could be heard suddenly underneath the Grand Easter Egg.

2 Garbuck Hobbs

The funny noise was made by an underground train. Inside the train was a man called Garbuck Hobbs. He was an inventor, too, but he wasn't a nice inventor like Professor Fred. He didn't make nice things like Easter eggs for the children of the town where he lived. He only made nasty things, like mouse-traps and bombs. He hated the Professor for being a better inventor than he was, so he meant to do something awful to the Bristleton Easter Egg and make her look silly.

Also, Garbuck Hobbs came from Bompton, so of course he didn't want Bristleton to win the football on Easter Monday. Bristleton had won it for – oh, at least two years. But Garbuck Hobbs was going to make sure Bompton won it this year.

Nobody knew he was in Bristleton. That was because he had dug himself a little house right underneath one of the goalposts of the football pitch.

Outside his front door he had built a railway line. The railway line went under

all the electric cables and the gas-pipes. It went under the water-pipes and the drains. It was so far underground that nobody could have dug it up by accident, not even when they were mending the road.

Just as Professor Fred and Little Fred had finished filling the Egg, he got into his underground train, which had just enough trucks behind it to carry an Egg-full of little chocolate elephants, and drove across Bristleton to the Town Hall.
He stopped just below where the Grand Easter Egg sat, waiting for tomorrow.

He had made a special periscope so

that he could see whether Professor Fred and Little Fred had finished filling the Grand Easter Egg with little chocolate elephants. There was no one there. He listened very hard, just in case Little

Fred or his granny had forgotten something and come back. There was no noise at all.

Garbuck Hobbs got out of his underground train. Then he picked up an enormous electric drill and began drilling.

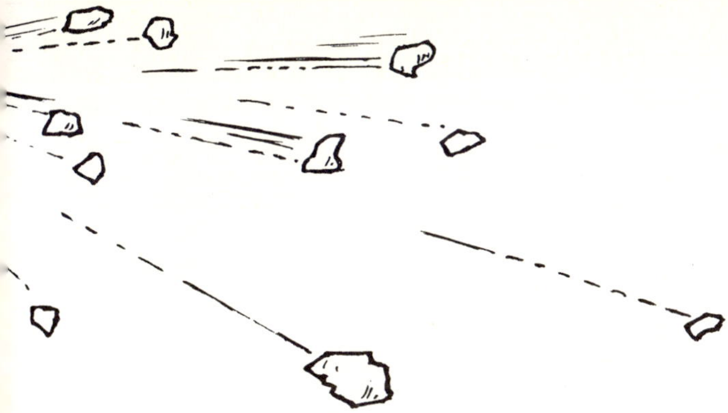

The drill went through lots of rock and earth and stone. Then something fell down that didn't look like rock or earth or stone. It was brown and shiny, with a squiggle of yellow icing on it.

Garbuck Hobbs picked it up and tasted it. 'Yummy,' he said. 'Mint chocolate.'

Then he put the drill away tidily into his underground train and waited.

Down through the hole fell thousands of little chocolate elephants, right into the trucks waiting for them.

Then as quick as a wink he made the train go backwards, all the way to his little house under the goalpost.

3 **Stolen!**

In the night Professor Fred heard a funny noise, right underneath her bed. She got out of bed and looked out of the window.

There was no one outside, everyone was asleep, so she went back to bed.

At about the same time Little Fred heard a funny noise, right underneath his bed. He got out and looked out of the window.

There was no one outside, everyone was asleep, so he went back to bed.

But in the morning Professor Fred called for her grandson.

'Think we'd better go and look at that Egg, Fred,' she said to Little Fred.

'Right ho, Granny,' said Little Fred.

When they unlocked the Town Hall door and switched the lights on, it all looked the same as last night.

'Nothing wrong, Granny,' said Little Fred.

'Doesn't look like it, Fred,' said Professor Fred. She tapped the Egg.

'You try, Fred,' she said.

Little Fred tapped.

'Nothing, Granny,' he said.

'Exactly, Fred,' said Professor Fred. 'There ought to be something. The Egg, Fred, is empty.'

'I think you're right,' said Little Fred sadly.

'Buck up, Fred,' said his granny. 'Look at this.' She got out a map and drew a line on it. It went from the Town Hall to the Bristleton football ground. 'Right underneath our houses, Fred,' she said.

'I thought I heard a train under my bed last night, Granny,' said Little Fred.

'I'll bet that's just what it was. An underground train. We'd better do something quickly.'

So they moved the Grand Easter Egg just a little bit, and climbed down the hole that Garbuck Hobbs had made with his drill.

'Just as I thought,' said Professor Fred. 'Somebody, Fred, is up to no good. Come on.'

It was a very long walk along the railway line, so it was afternoon by the time they reached Garbuck Hobbs' house under the goalpost. They hid behind one of the trucks and watched to see what would happen.

4 The Football Match

Outside, it was very hot. Everyone waved their football programmes in front of their faces to keep themselves cool.
The ground was packed.

Out came Bristleton football team. Everybody from Bristleton cheered like anything and waved their programmes, which had yellow and white stripes on them.

Out came Bompton football team. Everybody from Bompton cheered like anything and waved their programmes, which had blue and purple stripes on them.

Everybody, that is, except for Garbuck Hobbs and Professor Fred and Little Fred, because they were all underground.

The whistle blew and the game started.

You've never heard such a noise! Under the goalpost Garbuck Hobbs smiled a nasty smile because nobody would be able to hear him over all that row. He got out his electric drill and started to drill a hole through to the football ground, just big enough for a small chocolate elephant to get through.

Then, just as the Bristleton team had kicked the football right up near the goalpost, Garbuck Hobbs sent one of the chocolate elephants up in a specially invented lift.

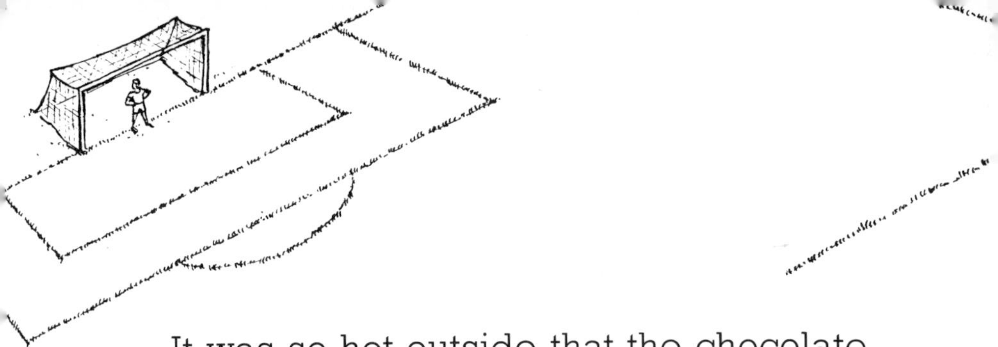

It was so hot outside that the chocolate elephant began to melt.

A Bristleton football player plonked a boot down on the melting elephant. Instead of kicking the ball right into the Bompton goal he skidded and fell over.

Then Garbuck Hobbs sent up lots more chocolate elephants and they too began to melt. Soon the Bristleton team were skidding all over the place. Every time the football came near Bompton's goal, someone slipped on a melting elephant and fell over.

The Bompton supporters cheered like anything. But the Bristleton supporters sat glumly in their seats, fanning themselves with white and yellow programmes.

Underground, Little Fred and his granny heard the row going on.

'Time we did something, Fred,' said Professor Fred.

'Right ho, Granny,' said Little Fred.

They nipped into Garbuck Hobbs' house when he wasn't looking and borrowed his electric drill. Then, while Garbuck Hobbs was laughing his head off right at the top of his lift, Little Fred jumped into the train and steered it along the tunnel to just underneath the Bristleton goal. Then he drilled, while his granny collected up the chocolate elephants that Garbuck Hobbs hadn't used yet.

'Right, chaps,' said Professor Fred, 'up you go.'

She didn't have a lift, but little Fred had

a very good catapult in his pocket.
Professor Fred passed the elephants,
and Little Fred twanged them right up the
hole they had made with the electric drill.

The Bompton team were kicking the football right down to the Bristleton end. Then a Bompton player plonked a boot down on a melting elephant. Instead of kicking the ball right into the Bristleton goal, he skidded, and fell over.

Now the Bristleton supporters cheered like anything. And the Bompton supporters sat glumly in their seats, fanning themselves with blue and purple programmes.

At half-time, nobody had got a goal at all, and the football pitch was horribly sticky with melted chocolate elephants.

'Time we went, Fred,' said Professor Fred.

'It's an awful waste of elephants,' said Little Fred sadly. He had sent one with his name on it up the hole to the pitch.

'Buck up, Fred,' said his granny. 'We've got more work to do.'

Fortunately, Garbuck Hobbs had gone back into his underground house, still chuckling, to eat a very large half-time ice-cream. So he didn't notice for some time that Professor Fred had pinched his train, and the rest of the elephants.

'Quick now, Fred. The sweeper.'

Little Fred knew exactly what his granny wanted. He jumped into the train and pressed a few buttons. The train rattled along the line to the Town Hall. Little Fred jumped out and found the big sweeping machine that they used for cleaning the Town Hall floor after Council meetings and children's parties. In no time at all he was back underneath the Bristleton goalposts.

'Up it goes, Fred,' said Professor Fred. 'Have the trucks ready.'

Outside, everyone was busy buying ice-creams, so they didn't see the Town Hall sweeper busily sweep all the sticky chocolate from the pitch.

'No time to lose,' said Professor Fred. 'Got to get back home double-quick.'

She sat next to him in the train and they rattled back to the hole under the Town Hall. Then they raced back to Professor Fred's house, turned on the machines at

ICES

double speed, poured in sackfuls of chocolate powder and worked like computers to make enough elephants to fill the Egg again.

"No time to make them trumpet the song, Fred,' said Professor Fred. 'Complicated clockwork, that.'

'There's still some old ones, Granny,' said Little Fred. 'I think there will be just enough.'

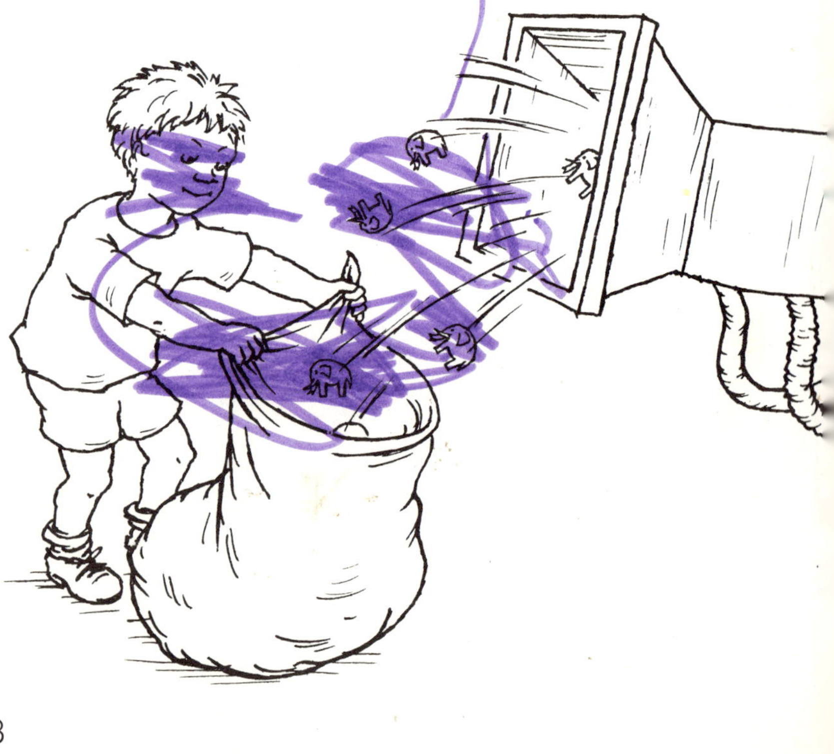

5 The Grand Opening

Garbuck Hobbs was in a very bad temper. Not only had someone come along and pinched back all the elephants and his train, but worse, Bristleton had won the football match.

All the Bompton fans went home, feeling very gloomy. But all the Bristleton people went to the Town Hall, and to the Grand Opening of the Grand Easter Egg.

The children of Bristleton, with their mums and dads, their uncles and aunts, and grannies and grandpas, waited in the enormous room.

'Okay, Fred,' said Professor Fred. 'Cut the ribbon.'

Little Fred went *snip-snap*, and the

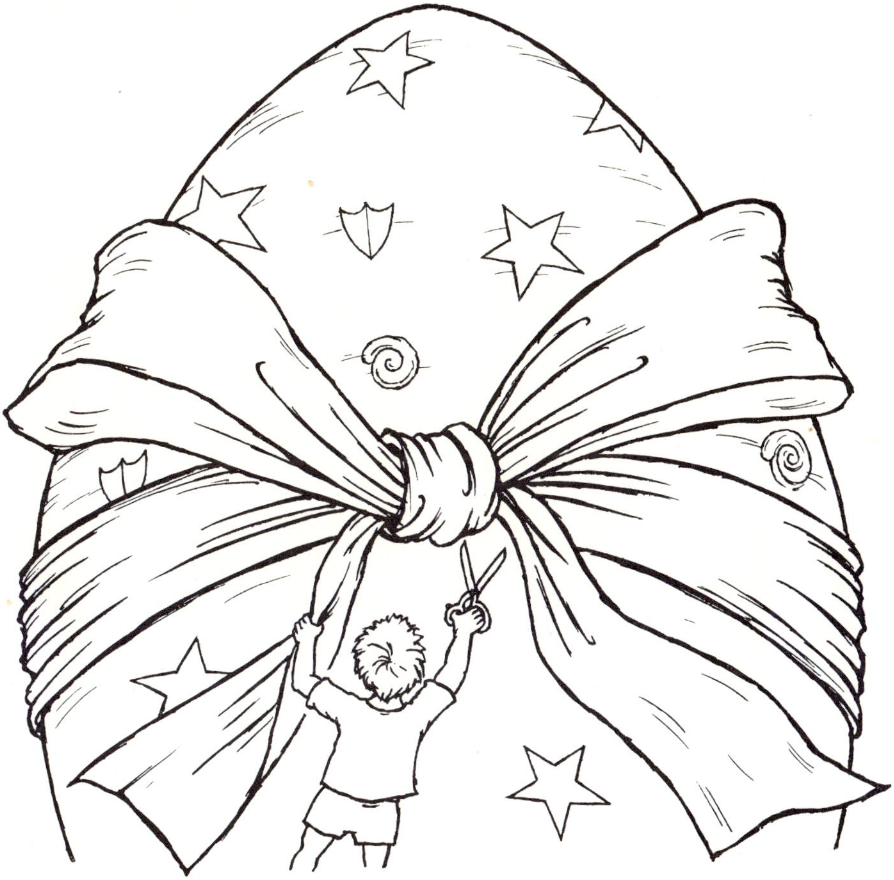

ribbon fell to the ground. The Grand Easter Egg went *crick-crack*, and the two halves fell to the floor.

And out of the Egg fell a herd of chocolate elephants. The front ones (just enough of them) lifted their trunks and trumpeted the Bristleton Football Club song in four parts. Everyone cheered madly, and the children raced to find the elephants with their names on.

Little Fred handed out pieces of the shell to the grown-ups. All the football team got a piece with a badge of the Bristleton Football Club on it.

And Little Fred had FOUR chocolate elephants, all with his name on them.

But there was someone standing in a corner who didn't get anything at all. It was Garbuck Hobbs.

Little Fred saw him and felt sorry for him. He walked over with his four elephants and held one of them out.

'Thank you for letting us borrow your train,' he said politely.

Garbuck Hobbs made a very rude noise. But he took Little Fred's chocolate elephant and popped it into his mouth, all in one go.

And he didn't even say thank you.

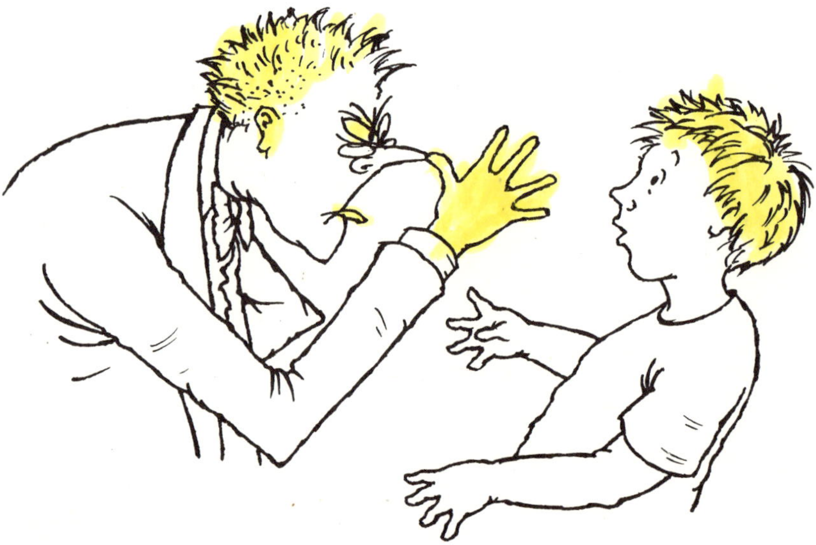